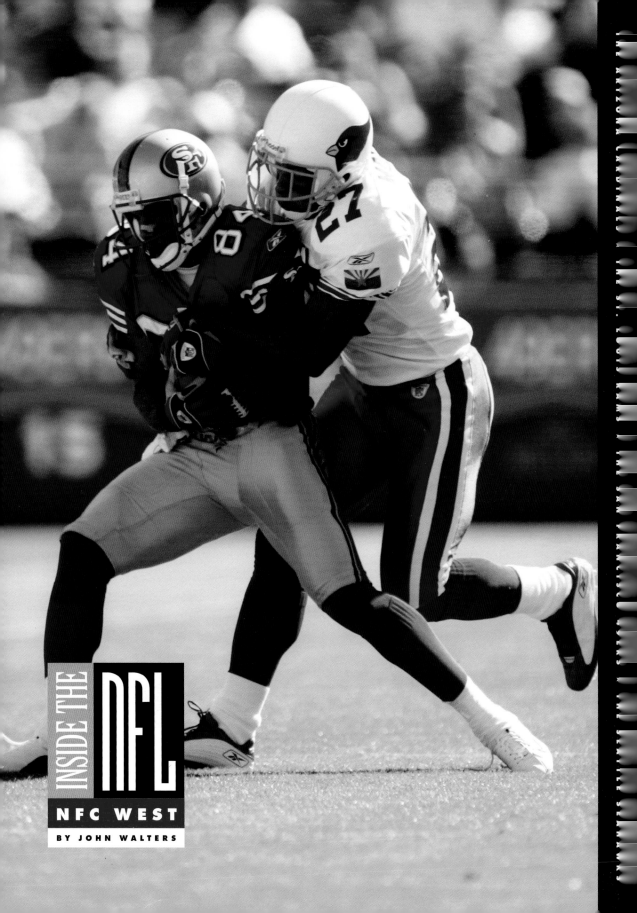

INSIDE THE **NFL**

NFC WEST

BY JOHN WALTERS

LIBRARY OF CONGRESS CATALOGING-IN-PUBLICATION DATA

Walters, John (John Andrew)
  NFC West / by John Walters.
    p. cm. — (Inside the NFL)
  Includes index.
    ISBN 1-59296-515-6 (library bound : alk. paper) 1. National Football League–
History–Juvenile literature. [1. National Football League–History.] I. Title: National
Football Conference West. II. Title. III. Child's World of sports. Inside the NFL
  GV955.5.N35W345 2006
  796.332'64'0973–dc22
                                        2005004807

ACKNOWLEDGEMENTS

The Child's World®: Mary Berendes, Publishing Director

Editorial Directions, Inc.: Russell Primm, Editorial Director and Line Editor; Matt
Messbarger, Project Editor; Elizabeth K. Martin, Assistant Editor; Olivia Nellums,
Editorial Assistant; Susan Hindman, Copy Editor; Susan Ashley, Beth Franken,
Proofreaders; Kevin Cunningham, Fact Checker; Tim Griffin/IndexServ, Indexer;
James Buckley Jr., Photo Researcher and Selector

The Design Lab: Kathleen Petelinsek, Design and Page Production

Photos: Cover: Ted S. Warren/AP
AP: 8, 20, 28; Bettmann/Corbis: 7, 10, 18, 25, 26; Scott Boehm/Getty: 2; Scott
Cunningham/Getty: 14; John Froschauer/AP: 39; Otto Greule/Allsport/Getty:
31; Tom Hauck/Getty: 41; Hulton Archive/Getty: 16; Robert Laberge/Getty:
1; Marcio Jose Sanchez/AP: 32; Sports Gallery/Al Messerschmidt: 11, 21, 27,
34, 35, 36, 37; Sports Gallery/Cleveland Press: 17; Keith Srakocic/AP: 13; Rick
Stewart/Getty: 22

Published in the United States of America by
The Child's World® • PO Box 326
Chanhassen, MN 55317-0326
800-599-READ • www.childsworld.com

NFC WEST

TABLE OF CONTENTS

INTRODUCTION

ARIZONA CARDINALS

Year Founded: 1920

**Home Stadium:
Sun Devil Stadium**

**Year Stadium
Opened: 1958**

**Team Colors: Red,
black, and white**

ST. LOUIS RAMS

Year Founded: 1937

**Home Stadium:
Edward Jones Dome**

**Year Stadium
Opened: 1995**

**Team Colors: Blue
and gold**

In 2002, the the National Football Conference (NFC) West said good-bye to three of its teams and welcomed two new ones. The radical change was a part of the league's **realignment,** in which the National Football League (NFL) switched from six divisions of five to six teams to eight divisions of four teams.

In the reshuffling, the NFC West lost the Atlanta Falcons, Carolina Panthers, and New Orleans Saints. It added the Arizona Cardinals and Seattle Seahawks.

The division kept its two most successful franchises. The St. Louis Rams won two NFL championships in the years before the **Super Bowl** existed and later won one Super Bowl. The San Francisco 49ers have the league's all-time best Super Bowl record, 5–0.

None of the four NFC West teams were born in the same **decade.** Two have been based in three states and, oddly, have the city of St. Louis in common.

Here are some beginner basics about our teams:

- The Arizona Cardinals are one of two remaining franchises (along with the Chicago Bears) that have been with the NFL since it began in 1920. They first played in Chicago.

- The St. Louis Rams began in 1937 as the Cleveland Rams. They later moved to Los Angeles. Then they moved a few miles down the California coast to Anaheim before moving east to St. Louis.

- The San Francisco 49ers were born in 1946 as part of the All-America Football Conference. They entered the NFL in 1950 and have always been based in San Francisco.

- The Seattle Seahawks entered the NFL in 1976. The club spent one season in the NFC West, then transferred to the AFC West for the next 25 seasons. Now, they have returned to the NFC West.

SAN FRANCISCO 49ERS

Year Founded: 1946

Home Stadium: Monster Park

Year Stadium Opened: 1960

Team Colors: Gold, red, and beige

SEATTLE SEAHAWKS

Year Founded: 1976

Home Stadium: Seahawks Stadium

Year Stadium Opened: 2002

Team Colors: Blue, navy, and green

CHAPTER ONE

THE ARIZONA CARDINALS

The NFL's oldest team is even older than the NFL itself. In 1898, the Morgan Athletic Club in Chicago began playing football. Two years later, its owner, Chris O'Brien, purchased used uniforms from the University of Chicago. Someone said the uniforms' maroon color appeared to have faded. "That's not maroon," O'Brien replied. "It's cardinal red." A team nickname was born.

In 1920, O'Brien paid $100 to enter the Cardinals into the brand-new American Professional Football Association (APFA). He then spent $3,000 to obtain star quarterback John "Paddy" Driscoll. Driscoll may have saved the franchise that year. The APFA had two Chicago teams, the Cardinals and the Tigers. The Cardinals won a key game between the two teams and became the fans' favorite. The Tigers closed down at the end of the season.

In 1921, the Decatur Staleys moved to Chicago, and a new city rivalry was born. The following year, the Staleys renamed themselves the Bears, and the APFA changed its name to the National Football League.

In 1929, the Bears and Cardinals met on Thanksgiving Day.

Ernie Nevers scored 40 points in a game in 1929.

Cardinals fullback Ernie Nevers scored six touch-downs. He also kicked four extra points, accounting for all of the Cardinals' points in the 40–6 win. That's still the NFL record for most points scored in a game by one player.

The Cardinals and Bears are the only original APFA franchises still in the NFL. Yet for all their history, the Cardinals have had little championship experience. In 1925, they were named NFL champions

The Bidwill family has owned the Cardinals since 1932. Charles Bidwill, who purchased the team for $50,000, died eight months before the Cardinals won the NFL title in 1947. His son Bill runs the team today.

Terry Metcalf was an electrifying runner.

after finishing with a league-best record of 11–2–1 (there were no playoffs then). In 1947, the Cardinals won their only NFL Championship Game, defeating the Philadelphia Eagles 28–21.

The Cardinals would not win another postseason game for 51 years. In the meantime, they moved twice. In 1960, the team moved to St. Louis, where it remained for 28 seasons. Some of the stars of that era were kicker Jim Bakken, quarterback Jim Hart, and running back Terry Metcalf. Bakken, the franchise's all-time leading scorer, made an NFL-record (since tied) seven field goals against the Steelers on September 24, 1967.

In 1974, St. Louis fielded one of its best teams. Hart led the NFC in touchdown passes (20). Metcalf led the conference in yards per carry (4.7)

Cardinals quarterback Jim Hardy had a wild two-game stretch in 1950. On September 24, he broke an NFL record when he was intercepted eight times in a 45–7 loss to Philadelphia. The next week, he bounced back to toss a club-record six touchdown passes in a 55–13 win over Baltimore.

Safety Larry Wilson (No. 8) had a Hall of Fame career from 1960 to 1972.

Pro Football Hall of Fame safety Larry Wilson spent 43 years with the Cardinals as a player and executive before retiring in 2003.

and was the NFL's top kick returner. St. Louis finished 10–4, but lost in the first round of the playoffs. The Cardinals were even better in 1975, finishing 11–3. Again they lost in the first round of the playoffs. The Cardinals would make only one postseason appearance—in the expanded playoffs of 1982—for the next 23 years.

Jim Hart passed for 34,639 yards in 18 seasons.

In 1988, the Cardinals relocated to Phoenix, Arizona. They've had only one winning season in the desert. It came in 1998. Guided by scrambling quarterback Jake "the Snake" Plummer, the Cardinals went 9–7. They beat Dallas in a wild-card playoff game for their first postseason win since 1947. The following week, Arizona lost to Minnesota in a divisional playoff game. In 2002, Arizona moved again, this time from the NFC East to the NFC West.

The change in divisions did not immediately produce a change in the Cardinals' fortunes. Arizona won only five games in 2002 and four in 2003, finishing in last place both seasons. But Cardinals fans hope to look back to 2004 as the year that marked a turning point in the resurgence of the franchise.

First, Dennis Green was hired as the head coach. Green, who had considerable success while leading the Minnesota Vikings through much of the 1990s, brought instant credibility and a winning attitude to Arizona. Then the Cardinals won six games in Green's first season. Though only a modest improvement over the previous year, Arizona escaped the cellar for the

It's no stretch to call the Cardinals' Anquan Boldin one of the NFL's top young pass catchers.

The Cardinals have high hopes under coach Dennis Green.

Emmitt Smith, the NFL's all-time leading rusher, signed with the Cardinals in 2003. He ran for only 256 yards that year, but bounced back to gain 937 yards in 2004.

first time since 2001, and the Cardinals remained in contention for a playoff berth until a loss to eventual division-champion Seattle in the next-to-last week of the season. Quarterback Josh McCown and receivers Anquan Boldin and Larry Fitzgerald gave Green a trio of young stars on offense around whom to build for the future.

CHAPTER TWO

THE ST. LOUIS RAMS

Those are ram horns painted on the sides of the St. Louis franchise's blue-and-gold helmets. You might say they are horns of plenty.

The Rams have won three NFL championships since entering the league as the Cleveland Rams in 1937. They have a tradition of winning seasons and dazzling players. The Rams' first NFL Most Valuable Player (MVP) was quarterback Bob Waterfield in 1945. It was Waterfield's first NFL season and the franchise's last in Cleveland. The Rams had suffered through seven seasons without a winning record in Ohio before Waterfield arrived. (Because of World War II, they did not field a team in 1943.)

Waterfield led the Cleveland Rams to a 9–1 record in his rookie season. In the NFL Championship Game, played on an icy field in Cleveland's Municipal Stadium, the Rams nipped the Washington Redskins, 15–14.

The following season, the Rams moved to Los Angeles. They

Pete Rozelle was hired as a member of the Rams' public-relations staff in 1952. He became NFL commissioner in 1960, a job he held for nearly three decades. Rozelle is credited with turning the NFL into America's most popular spectator sport.

Bob Waterfield was one of the Rams' early stars.

became the first of many pro sports franchises to **migrate** to California. From nearby University of California, Los Angeles (UCLA), they signed Kenny Washington and Woody Strode, the first two African Americans to play in the NFL since 1933.

By 1950, the Rams seemed to have as many famous players as MGM Studios. Besides Waterfield, the Rams boasted quarterback Norm Van Brocklin and receivers Tom Fears and Elroy "Crazylegs" Hirsch. "Crazylegs" was very popular with fans. As he tried to run off the field after the final game of his career in 1957, he was mobbed. Fans ripped off parts of his uniform for souvenirs.

The Rams were a record-setting machine in the early 1950s. Fears caught 84 passes in 1950, including 18 in a single game. Both were NFL records. Van

Speedy and elusive Elroy Hirsch was nicknamed Crazylegs.

Merlin Olsen (No. 74) was fearsome on the field—not so off it.

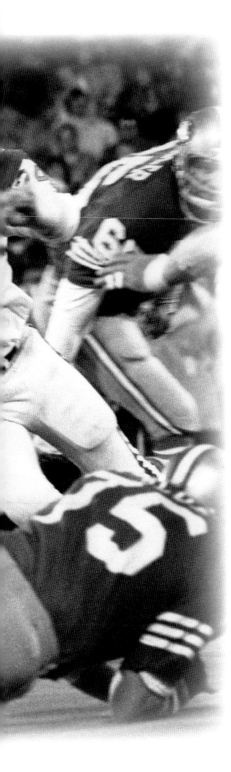

Brocklin, who shared quarterback duties with Waterfield for a few seasons, passed for an NFL single-game record 554 yards in a 54–14 defeat of the New York Yanks in 1951.

The Rams played the Cleveland Browns in the NFL Championship Game in both 1950 and 1951. The Browns won the first meeting, 30–28.

In the rematch the next season, Van Brocklin connected with Fears on a 73-yard, game-winning touchdown pass. The game was the first NFL contest televised coast-to-coast.

Roman Gabriel was the Rams' next great quarterback. In 1969, he led Los Angeles to 11 straight wins and was named league MVP. The heart of the Rams in the 1960s, however, was their defensive line. "The Fearsome Foursome," as they were known, consisted of Roosevelt Grier, Deacon Jones, Lamar Lundy, and Merlin Olsen.

Several Rams have had successful acting careers. Fred Dryer starred in the title role of the detective series *Hunter* in the 1980s. Merlin Olsen appeared not so fearsome as Jonathan Garvey in the hit series *Little House on the Prairie* in the 1970s.

The Rams gave the favored Steelers all they could handle in Super Bowl XIV,
though Pittsburgh ultimately prevailed.

In the 1970s, the Rams were a model of success
and frustration. Los Angeles finished in first place in
the NFC West each year from 1973 to 1979. Defensive
ends Jack Youngblood and Fred Dryer led a Ram-
tough defense that in 1975 allowed only 135 points.
That was the second fewest in league history for a
14-game season; NFL teams today play 16 games.

The Rams played the Steelers in Super Bowl XIV
after the 1979 season. The Rams were a heavy under-

Marshall Faulk was the last piece to the Super Bowl puzzle in 1999.

Marc Bulger is the latest quarterback sensation for the Rams.

dog but led in the fourth quarter before losing, 31–19.
In 1984, the Rams moved 50 miles (80.5 kilometers)
south to Anaheim (they kept the name Los Angeles).
Second-year running back Eric Dickerson ran almost
as far. Dickerson, who a year earlier had gained an
NFL rookie-record 1,808 yards, this time ran for an
NFL single-season-record 2,105 yards.

The Rams moved yet again in 1995. This time, the franchise
moved east, to St. Louis. After nine straight losing seasons, the Rams
broke out in 1999. First-year starting quarterback Kurt Warner led
the franchise to a 13–3 record. Then the Rams beat the Tennessee
Titans, 23–16, in Super Bowl XXXIV.

The Rams' offense became known as "The Greatest Show on
Turf." Warner was named league MVP in 1999 and in 2001 (a
season in which St. Louis went 14–2). Running back Marshall Faulk
was the MVP in 2000, when he scored an NFL-record 26 touchdowns.

In the six-season span beginning in 1999, the Rams won three
division titles and made the playoffs on two other occasions. They
reached the Super Bowl again in 2001, but were upset by the New
England Patriots in game XXXVI.

By 2004, Warner had left to join the New York Giants, and
Faulk began giving way to rookie star Steven Jackson. But with
Marc Bulger as quarterback and explosive veterans Torry Holt and
Isaac Bruce catching the ball, St. Louis still struck fear in opposing
defenses around the league. The Rams earned a wild-card berth that
year with a win over the playoff-bound New York Jets on the final
weekend of the regular season.

CHAPTER THREE

THE SAN FRANCISCO 49ERS

Jerry Rice and the Golden Gate Bridge are the greatest links in San Francisco. The beautiful suspension bridge connects the city to Marin County. Rice, the greatest wide receiver in NFL history, connects the careers of 49ers quarterbacks Joe Montana and Steve Young.

Montana and Young, both of whom found Rice to be their favorite target, guided San Francisco to five Super Bowl victories between 1981 and 1994. In that stretch, the 49ers were as successful as any other franchise in professional sports.

It was not always that way. The 49ers were born in 1946 as a member of the All-America Football Conference (AAFC). In each of their four seasons in that league, the 49ers finished second to the Cleveland Browns.

Fullback Joe "The Jet" Perry was the star. The franchise's first African American player, Perry scampered 58 yards on his first career carry. In 16 pro seasons from 1948 to 1963, Perry would rush for 9,723 yards.

In 1950, the AAFC disbanded. Three of its teams—the Browns, 49ers, and Baltimore Colts—were **annexed** by the NFL. San Francisco

Joe (The Jet) Perry got his nickname for his fast starts off the snap.

was an exciting team to watch. In the early 1950s, the 49ers boasted the "Million-Dollar Backfield" of Perry, John Henry Johnson, and Hugh McElhenny.

The term was a big exaggeration—few players earned more than $10,000 per season then—but this trio was money. In 1952, McElhenny was the NFL Player of the Year, and in 1954 Perry and Johnson finished one-two in the league in rushing.

In 1957, the 49ers had their hearts broken. They

In 1957, quarterback Y. A. Tittle and receiver R. C. Owens developed the "Alley-Oop" pass. Tittle would arch a high throw and allow the six-foot-three Owens to outjump defenders for the ball.

Hugh McElhenny was a dazzling runner fans called "The King."

tied Detroit for first place in the Western Conference. The teams met in a playoff for the right to face Cleveland in the NFL Championship Game. Behind future Hall of Famer Y.A. Tittle's passing, San Francisco jumped to a 24–7 halftime lead. The Lions staged an incredible second-half rally, however, and won 31–27.

No 49ers team would make the postseason again until 1970. Then, more heartbreak awaited. Each year from 1970 to 1972, the Dallas Cowboys knocked San

John Brodie was the NFL MVP in 1970.

Quarterback Joe Montana and coach Bill Walsh gave 49ers' fans plenty to smile about during their time together in San Francisco.

Francisco out of the playoffs. The third loss hurt the worst. Playing at home, the 49ers led 28–13 in the fourth quarter. Then Roger Staubach led the Cowboys to a field goal and a pair of touchdowns to win, 30–28.

In a city famous for earthquakes, San Francisco did not produce even a tremor the rest of the 1970s. The 49ers were a miserable 2–14 in both 1978 and 1979. However, two good things happened in 1979: the 49ers hired Bill Walsh as head coach, and Walsh drafted quarterback Joe Montana from Notre Dame.

Montana was supposedly too slow, too small, and too weak-armed to make it in the NFL. Doubts remained until December 7, 1980. On that afternoon, the 49ers trailed the New Orleans Saints, 35–7, at halftime. Montana took the 49ers on four long touchdown drives to tie the score. Ray Wersching's field goal in overtime ended it, 38–35. The 49ers had the greatest regular-season comeback win in NFL history. Montana had arrived.

The 49ers owned the rest of the decade. In 1981, they exacted revenge on the Cowboys in the NFC Championship Game. In the final minute, Montana tossed to a leaping Dwight Clark in the end zone for a 28–27 victory. The play is known simply as "The Catch."

San Francisco won Super Bowl XVI (over the Cincinnati Bengals, 26–21) to cap the 1981 season and Super Bowl XIX (over the Miami Dolphins, 38–16) to cap the 1984 season. Then Jerry Rice arrived, and the 49ers really became dangerous.

Rice is the best wide receiver, if not overall player, ever to grace the NFL. He has caught more passes for more yards and more touchdowns than anyone else in history. Rice played 16 seasons in San Francisco (1985–2000) before crossing the bay to Oakland in 2001.

Montana and Rice teamed up to help the 49ers to another pair of Super Bowl wins. San Francisco beat Cincinnati 20–16 in Super Bowl XXIII to close the 1988 season, then routed Denver 55–10 the next year.

In all, Montana won four Super Bowls. He never threw an interception in the big game and was named Super Bowl MVP three times.

In 1991, Steve Young took over as the 49ers' starting quarterback. Young continued San Francisco's run of success. Montana had been league MVP twice. Young also would become a two-time league MVP. Montana had thrown five touchdown passes in a Super Bowl, three of them to Rice. Young tossed six touchdown passes while leading the 49ers to the

Steve DeBerg is the greatest warm-up act in NFL history. DeBerg was replaced at quarterback in San Francisco by Montana, then in Denver by John Elway, and finally in Tampa Bay by Steve Young (before he joined the 49ers). Still, DeBerg, who started for the Atlanta Falcons in 1999 at age 45, is in the NFL's top 20 in career passing yardage.

franchise's fifth Super Bowl win, a 49–26 spanking of the San Diego Chargers in Super Bowl XXIX. Three of Young's six touchdown passes went to Rice.

The 49ers haven't been back to the Super Bowl since. Young retired after the 1999 season and Rice left via free agency following the 2000 season. Although San Francisco did reach the postseason six times in the eight-season span from 1995 to

Joe Montana was nearly flawless in four Super Bowls. He completed 68.0 percent of his passes for 1,142 yards and 11 touchdowns, with no interceptions.

Jerry Rice amassed unbelievable statistics in his 16 seasons with the 49ers.

San Francisco owner John York (left) handed the coaching reins to Mike Nolan in 2005.

The 49ers hired Mike Nolan as head coach in 2005. He is the son of Dick Nolan, who was the club's head coach from 1968 to 1975.

2002, the proud franchise won only seven games in 2003. Then, with a team hamstrung by salary-cap constraints and virtually devoid of stars, the 49ers hit rock bottom the next year. They dropped to 2–14, the worst record in the league.

CHAPTER FOUR

THE SEATTLE SEAHAWKS

The NFL already had franchises in New England, Miami, and San Diego. In 1976, the league expanded to the fourth corner of the continental United States by awarding a franchise to Seattle. The Seahawks entered the NFL as an expansion team, along with the Tampa Bay Buccaneers, in the nation's **bicentennial** year. Seattle was placed in the NFC West, then moved to the AFC West in 1977. In 2002, the Seahawks returned to the NFC West.

Seattle lost the first five games in franchise history, then defeated Tampa Bay 13–10 on October 17, 1976, for its first victory. Seattle won one more game during its initial season. The Seahawks defeated the Atlanta Falcons, 30–13, at home in the Kingdome in front of 60,000 raucous fans.

No one expects an expansion team to be good. Seattle met expectations that first season. The Seahawks' defense finished last in points allowed and yards allowed. Rookie quarterback Jim Zorn, a scrambling **southpaw,** threw 27 interceptions in that 2–12 season.

Seattle quickly improved, however. The Seahawks finished 9–7 in 1978, their third season. No third-year expansion team had ever finished with a better record. Zorn, having found a go-to receiver in future Hall of Famer Steve Largent, led the AFC in pass completions (248) and yardage (3,283). Largent caught 71 passes, also tops in the conference. Fullback David Sims led the AFC with 15 touchdowns, but was forced to retire the following year due to a neck injury.

Jim Zorn made the Seahawks' offense a force from the start.

Kenny Easley was an intimidating safety.

The Seahawks made their first great draft pick in 1981, selecting UCLA All-American safety Kenny Easley. Seattle was still too thin on defense, however, and finished in last place in the AFC West for the second straight season.

During the 1982 NFL players' strike, head coach Jack Patera was fired. Patera had been the Seahawks' only coach until then. In 1983, Chuck Knox, who had won six division titles with the Los Angeles Rams and Buffalo Bills in the last decade, became head coach.

Dave Krieg may be the most underrated quarterback in NFL history. Though his name is never mentioned among the all-time greats, Krieg ranks in the NFL's all-time top 10 in completions, attempts, yardage, and touchdown passes.

In 1984, the Seahawks retired the jersey No.12. The number did not represent a player, but rather the "12th Man," meaning the fans. Seattle's deafening fans could make the Kingdome an intimidating place for opponents.

Knox was dedicated to establishing a rushing attack in Seattle. His offense became known as "Ground Chuck." Its **cornerstone** was running back Curt Warner from Penn State. Warner had a fantastic rookie season. He led the AFC in rushing with 1,449 yards, as the Seahawks qualified for their first playoff berth.

Another new face on offense was Dave Krieg. An unlikely NFL star, Krieg had played at tiny Milton College, a school that no longer even existed. He was efficient and effective, though. In Seattle's first

Curt Warner made Seattle's "Ground Chuck" go.

Sure-handed Steve Largent caught 819 passes in his career.

postseason game, Krieg completed 12 of 13 passes for 200 yards and three touchdowns. Seattle wiped out the Broncos, 31–7.

Seattle surprised the NFL yet again the following week. Warner rushed for 113 yards as the Seahawks upset the Miami Dolphins on the road, 27–20. Suddenly, the Seahawks found themselves in the AFC Championship Game against the Los Angeles Raiders. The dream ended in Southern California. The Raiders won, 30–14.

Seattle won its season-opener for the first time in franchise history in 1984. The Seahawks beat the Cleveland Browns, 33–0, but paid a huge price for the win. Warner suffered a season-ending knee injury. Still, Seattle went on to finish 12–4 that year, its best record ever. Easley was named NFL Defensive Player of the Year.

Seattle hosted the defending Super Bowl-champion Raiders in the wild-card game. The Seahawks won, 13–7, in front of the frenzied Kingdome fans. The next weekend, the Seahawks lost at Miami, 31–10.

By 1986, Warner was back to his old self. He led the AFC in rushing with a career-high 1,481 yards. Seattle finished 10–6 but in third place in the strong AFC West.

The Seahawks made the playoffs in 1987 and 1988, but met only misery, losing their first game each time.

Largent retired in 1989. Not very fast and not 6 feet (183 centimeters) tall, Largent retired with 819 career catches and with at least

> **Steve Largent was elected to the U.S. House of Representatives in 1994. Representing his home state, Oklahoma, Largent served seven years in Congress before resigning in 2001 to run for governor of Oklahoma. In the 2002 election, Largent, a Republican, lost to Democrat Brad Henry by less than 7,000 votes out of more than 1 million cast.**

Quarterback Jon Kitna and the Seahawks made the playoffs in 1999, but couldn't get past the Miami Dolphins.

one reception in 177 consecutive games. Both were records then, though both have since been broken by Jerry Rice.

The Seahawks had few highlights in the 1990s. They made the playoffs only once all decade, in 1999, losing to Miami in the first round.

The Seahawks unveiled new uniforms in 2002. It was the first significant uniform change in the club's 26-year history.

The Kingdome, Seattle's only home until then, was demolished following the 1999 season. After playing two seasons at the University of Washington's Husky Stadium, Seattle moved into brand-new Seahawks Stadium in 2002.

On September 29, in front of a national television audience on ESPN, running back Shaun Alexander ran for five touchdowns in the first half against the Vikings. A year earlier, also on an ESPN Sunday-night telecast, Alexander galloped for 266 yards and three touchdowns against the Raiders.

That was just a preview of things to come. In 2004, Alexander rushed for a career-best 1,696 yards and scored 20 touchdowns to help the Seahawks win the NFC West for the first time.

It was the third time in the six seasons since Mike Holmgren took over as head coach in 1999 that Seattle had reached the playoffs. But also for the third time, the Seahawks lost in the opening round. A narrow, 27–20 loss to division-rival St. Louis left Seattle still seeking its first postseason victory since 1984.

Shawn Alexander missed winning his first NFL rushing title by the narrowest of margins in 2004. With 1,696 yards, he finished just one yard behind the New York Jets' Curtis Martin.

Shaun Alexander is one of the NFL's dominant runners.

STAT STUFF

T E A M   R E C O R D S

TEAM	ALL-TIME RECORD	NFL TITLES (MOST RECENT)	NUMBER OF TIMES IN PLAYOFFS	TOP COACH (WINS)
Arizona	446–627–39	2 (1947)	7	Don Coryell (42)
St. Louis	484–423–20	3 (1999)	27	John Robinson (79)
San Francisco	472–361–15	5 (1994)	23	George Seifert (108)
Seattle	214–238–0	0	7	Chuck Knox (83)

M E M B E R S   O F   T H E   P R O   F O O T B A L L   H A L L   O F   F A M E

SAN FRANCISCO PLAYER	POSITION	DATE INDUCTED
Jimmy Johnson	Cornerback	1994
John Henry Johnson	Fullback	1987
Ronnie Lott	Cornerback/Safety	2000
Hugh McElhenny	Halfback	1970
Joe Montana	Quarterback	2002
Leo Nomellini	Defensive Tackle	1969
Joe Perry	Fullback	1969
Bob St. Clair	Tackle	1990
O. J. Simpson	Running Back	1985
Y. A. Tittle	Quarterback	1971
Bill Walsh	Coach	1993
Dave Wilcox	Linebacker	2000
Steve Young	Quarterback	2005

SEATTLE PLAYER	POSITION	DATE INDUCTED
Carl Eller	Defensive End	2004
Franco Harris	Running Back	1990
Steve Largent	Wide Receiver	1995

MEMBERS OF THE PRO FOOTBALL HALL OF FAME

ARIZONA PLAYER	POSITION	DATE INDUCTED
Charles W. Bidwill Jr.	Owner	1967
Guy Chamberlin	End	1965
Jimmy Conzelman	Quarterback	1964
Dan Dierdorf	Tackle	1996
John (Paddy) Driscoll	Quarterback	1965
Walt Kiesling	Guard/Coach	1966
Earl (Curly) Lambeau	Coach	1963
Dick (Night Train) Lane	Cornerback	1974
Ollie Matson	Halfback	1972
Don Maynard	Wide Receiver	1987
Ernie Nevers	Fullback	1963
Jackie Smith	Tight End	1994
Jim Thorpe	Halfback	1963
Charley Trippi	Halfback/Quarterback	1968
Larry Wilson	Safety	1978

ST. LOUIS PLAYER	POSITION	DATE INDUCTED
George Allen	Coach	2002
Bob Brown	Tackle	2004
Eric Dickerson	Running Back	1999
Tom Fears	End	1970
Bill George	Linebacker	1974
Sid Gillman	Coach	1983
Elroy (Crazylegs) Hirsch	Halfback/End	1968
David (Deacon) Jones	Defensive End	1980
Dick (Night Train) Lane	Cornerback	1974
Tom Mack	Guard	1999
Ollie Matson	Halfback	1972
Tommy McDonald	Wide Receiver	1998
Joe Namath	Quarterback	1985
Merlin Olsen	Defensive Tackle	1982
Dan Reeves	Owner	1967
Andy Robustelli	Defensive End	1971
Texas E. (Tex) Schramm	President/General Manager	1991
Jackie Slater	Tackle	2001
Norm Van Brocklin	Quarterback	1971
Bob Waterfield	Quarterback	1965
Ron Yary	Tackle	2001
Jack Youngblood	Defensive End	2001

MORE STAT STUFF

N F C   W E S T   C A R E E R   L E A D E R S   (T H R O U G H   2 0 0 4)

ARIZONA

CATEGORY	NAME (YEARS WITH TEAM)	TOTAL
Rushing	Ottis Anderson (1979–1986)	7,999
Passing yards	Jim Hart (1966–1983)	34,639
Touchdown passes	Jim Hart (1966–1983)	209
Receptions	Larry Centers (1990–98)	535
Touchdowns	Roy Green (1979–1990)	70
Scoring	Jim Bakken (1962–1978)	1,380

ST. LOUIS

CATEGORY	NAME (YEARS WITH TEAM)	TOTAL
Rushing	Eric Dickerson (1983–87)	7,245
Passing yards	Jim Everett (1986–1993)	23,758
Touchdown passes	Roman Gabriel (1962–1972)	154
Receptions	Isaac Bruce (1994–2004)	777
Touchdowns	Marshall Faulk (1999–2004)	84
Scoring	Jeff Wilkins (1997–2004)	878

SAN FRANCISCO

CATEGORY	NAME (YEARS WITH TEAM)	TOTAL
Rushing	Joe Perry (1950–1960, 1963)	7,344
Passing yards	Joe Montana (1979–1992)	35,124
Touchdown passes	Joe Montana (1979–1992)	244
Receptions	Jerry Rice (1985–2000)	1,281
Touchdowns	Jerry Rice (1985–2000)	187
Scoring	Jerry Rice (1985–2000)	1,130

SEATTLE

CATEGORY	NAME (YEARS WITH TEAM)	TOTAL
Rushing	Chris Warren (1990–97)	6,706
Passing yards	Dave Krieg (1980–1991)	26,132
Touchdown passes	Dave Krieg (1980–1991)	195
Receptions	Steve Largent (1976–1989)	819
Touchdowns	Steve Largent (1976–1989)	101
Scoring	Norm Johnson (1982–1990)	810

GLOSSARY

annexed—incorporated or combined into an existing group

bicentennial—the 200th anniversary (in this case, of America's independence)

cornerstone—a vital or fundamental part of something

decade—any 10-year period, such as the 1980s

migrate—to move from one region to another

realignment—a change in the way something is organized

southpaw—a slang term for a left-hander

Super Bowl—the NFL's annual championship game, played in late January or early February at a different stadium each year

TIME LINE

1920 Chicago Cardinals become charter members of the NFL

1925 Cardinals are named NFL champions after going 11–2–1

1937 Rams begin play in Cleveland

1946 San Francisco 49ers are founded as part of the All-America Football Conference (AAFC); Cleveland shifts its franchise to Los Angeles

1947 Cardinals win the NFL Championship Game for the first, and only, time

1950 The AAFC folds, but the 49ers join the NFL

1951 Los Angeles Rams win their first league championship

1960 Chicago Cardinals move to St. Louis

1976 Seattle Seahawks join the NFL as an expansion team

1981 San Francisco wins the first of five Super Bowls in a 14-season span

1988 Cardinals move to Arizona and become the Phoenix Cardinals

1994 Cardinals are renamed the Arizona Cardinals

1995 Los Angeles Rams move to St. Louis

1999 Rams win Super Bowl XXXIV, their first NFL title in 48 years

2004 Seahawks win the NFC West for the first time

FOR MORE INFORMATION ABOUT

THE NFC WEST AND THE NFL

B O O K S

Bell, Lonnie. *The History of the San Francisco 49ers*. Mankato, Minn.:
   Creative Education, 2005.

Bell, Lonnie. *The History of the St. Louis Rams*. Mankato, Minn.:
   Creative Education, 2005.

Buckley, James Jr., and Jerry Rice. *America's Greatest Game*. New York:
   Hyperion Books for Children, 1998.

Christopher, Matt. *In the Huddle with . . . Steve Young*. Boston: Little
   Brown and Co., 1996.

Gilbert, Sara. *The History of the Arizona Cardinals*. Mankato, Minn.:
   Creative Education, 2005.

Gilbert, Sara. *The History of the Seattle Seahawks*. Mankato, Minn.:
   Creative Education, 2005.

Ramen, Fred. *Joe Montana.* New York: Rosen Publishing Group, 2003.

O N   T H E   W E B

Visit our home page for lots of links about the NFC West:
http://www.childsworld.com/links

Note to Parents, Teachers, and Librarians: We routinely verify our Web links to make
sure they are safe, active sites—so encourage your readers to check them out!

INDEX

A B O U T   T H E   A U T H O R

John Walters is a former staff writer at *Sports Illustrated* who worked at the magazine from 1989 to 2001. He has also written two books, *Basketball for Dummies,* which he co-wrote with former Notre Dame basketball coach Digger Phelps, and *The Same River Twice: A Season with Geno Auriemma and the Connecticut Huskies,* which chronicles the women's basketball team's 2000–2001 season.